The Story of Jonah

First published in 1999 by Franklin Watts
96 Leonard Street, London EC2A 4XD

Franklin Watts Australia
14 Mars Road
Lane Cove
NSW 2066

Paperback edition 2000

Series editor: Rachel Cooke
Art director: Robert Walster
Consultants: Reverend Richard Adfield;
Laurie Rosenberg, Board of Deputies of British Jews

A CIP catalogue record for this book
is available from the British Library.

ISBN 0 7496 3213 5 (hbk); 0 7496 3795 1 (pbk)

Dewey Classification 221

Printed in Hong Kong/China

The Story of Jonah

Retold by Mary Auld

Illustrated by Diana Mayo

W

FRANKLIN WATTS

NEW YORK • LONDON • SYDNEY

Long ago in the land of Canaan there lived a man called Jonah. He was a prophet and God often spoke to him.

One day God told Jonah to go to the great city of Nineveh. "The people there are full of wickedness," He said. "You must tell them to change their ways."

But Jonah ran away from God. He
went to the port of Joppa and found a
boat that was about to sail to a place far
from Nineveh. The sailors would take
him with them - for a fee. So he paid his
fare and clambered on board.

The boat had not sailed far, when
God sent a great wind across the sea.
The wind pushed up huge waves,
which battered against the boat and
threatened to break it to pieces.

The sailors were afraid. The boat
was laden with goods to sell and
now they threw these into the sea.
Perhaps the lighter boat would ride
the waves more easily.

 7

All this while, Jonah was sleeping
below deck.

The captain came to him. "Wake up,
wake up," he shouted. "How can you
sleep through this storm? You must
pray to your God to save us all."

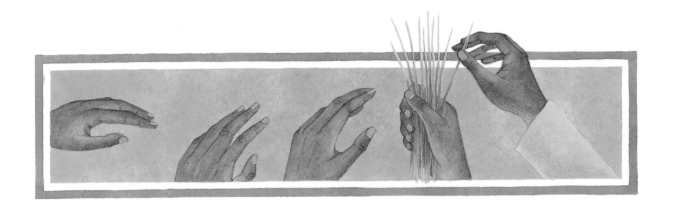

Jonah joined the other sailors and they drew lots to see who had provoked so great a storm. Jonah drew the shortest lot. "You have caused this rage," said the sailors. "But what have you done?"

"I am a Hebrew," Jonah replied. "And I worship the Lord, the maker of land and sea. And now I am running away from Him."

The sailors were terrified. "What must we do to calm the sea?"

"You must throw me overboard," said Jonah. "It is the only way to make the storm die down. It's my fault that you are in danger."

The sailors didn't want to kill Jonah. They tried all the harder to row back to land, but they could not. The storm grew even wilder than before.

Exhausted, the men cried out to God: "Oh Lord, please don't punish us for killing this innocent man. We are only doing as you wanted." And they took Jonah and threw him overboard.

Immediately, the sea became calm
and the wind died away. The sailors
were amazed by God's power. They
made a sacrifice to Him and offered
prayers of thanks.

Jonah sank deep beneath the waves. But God did not mean Jonah to die. He sent a great fish which swallowed the prophet whole. And so Jonah found himself sitting inside the belly of a fish.

For three day and three nights, Jonah lay in his strange, dark prison. And all the while he prayed to God.

"Lord, you have thrown me into the deep and out of your sight. Yet still I pray to you. The waters surrounded me, seaweed wrapped itself around my head and I thought I was lost forever. But you have saved me. I remembered you, and I prayed to you. And now I thank you and I swear I will do as I have promised. Only the Lord can save."

And the Lord spoke to the fish and it threw up Jonah, out of its belly and on to dry land.

God spoke to Jonah again, telling
him to go to Nineveh. And this time
Jonah did as he was told.

Now Nineveh was a huge city - so
large that it would take a man three
days to walk around it. Jonah did not

hesitate. He went straight into the heart of the city and called out the Lord's message. "Stop your evil and violent ways. If you do not, in forty days Nineveh will be completely destroyed," he warned.

So the people of Nineveh believed Jonah and God's word. Everyone, from the richest to the poorest, put on rough sackcloth, and began to fast - not a crumb of bread, not a drop of water passed their lips.

Even the king of Nineveh took off his golden robes and dressed in sackcloth. And he sat in ashes rather than on his throne.

The king and his people cried out to the Lord. "We will turn away from violence and our evil ways. Oh spare us, mighty God, from your fierce anger."

And God saw what they had done and heard their prayers. And He spared the city from destruction.

Jonah wasn't happy with God's decision. In fact, he was furious. He could not understand why God had shown such mercy to the people of Nineveh.

"Why have you been so kind?" he shouted at God. "This is why I didn't want to come to Nineveh - I knew you would change your mind, for you are too full of goodness.

"You should kill me now, Lord. I would rather be dead than alive!" he cried out in his fury.

The Lord only said, "Are you right to be angry?"

So Jonah went east out of the
city. He built a rough shelter and sat
beneath it, and watched the city and
waited. Would the Lord take any
notice of his wishes?

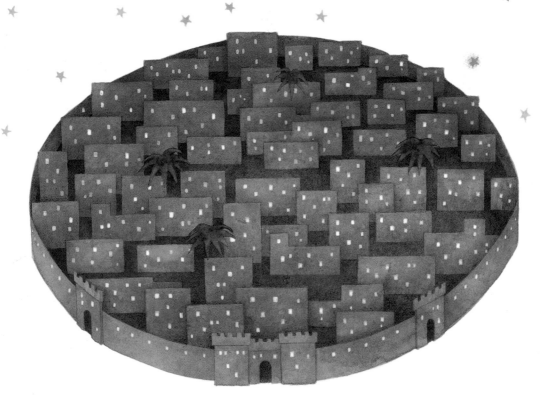

The city slept peacefully. During the
night, at God's command, an amazing
vine grew up over Jonah's shelter.

All through the day that followed,
the vine shaded Jonah from the heat
of the sun. The prophet was delighted.

 23

The next day the vine was dead. God had sent a worm in the night and it had eaten the plant so that it withered away.

The day was extremely hot and windy. The sun beat down on Jonah's head and he felt faint with heat. Jonah's anger returned. "I am better off dead than alive!" he said again.

And God asked Jonah, "Are you right to be angry that the vine has died?"

"Yes, I am right," said Jonah. "The vine was a good thing."

And God explained his actions to Jonah.

"Why do you feel sorry about the vine dying? You didn't plant it and you did nothing to make it grow. It came in the night and died in the night.

And yet the great city of Nineveh stands. Isn't it better that I should spare the lives of twelve thousand people than that of a single vine?"

About this story

The Story of Jonah is a retelling of the Book of Jonah, one of the books that make up the Bible. The Bible is the name given to the collection of writings that are sacred, in different forms, to the Jewish and Christian religions. The Book of Jonah is one of the 39 books in the Hebrew Bible or Christian Old Testament.

Who was Jonah?

The Book of Jonah was written about 2300 years ago. It was not written by Jonah, who probably lived several hundred years before that. It is hard to give exact dates and background details to the events in the Book of Jonah and most people believe the story's importance is in its religious meaning rather than as a historical record.

Very little is known about Jonah himself. He is mentioned only once before in the Bible (2 Kings 14: 25). He was a prophet who lived in Gath-hepher, a small village near Nazareth in Canaan.

Where was Nineveh?

The map opposite shows the whereabouts of the places mentioned in the Book of Jonah including the city of Nineveh. Nineveh was a major city of the Assyrian Empire and its capital from about 700 to 612 BC, when the city was destroyed by Babylonian armies from the south. The Assyrian Empire was an important power in the Middle East through much of early Jewish history and is frequently mentioned in the Bible.

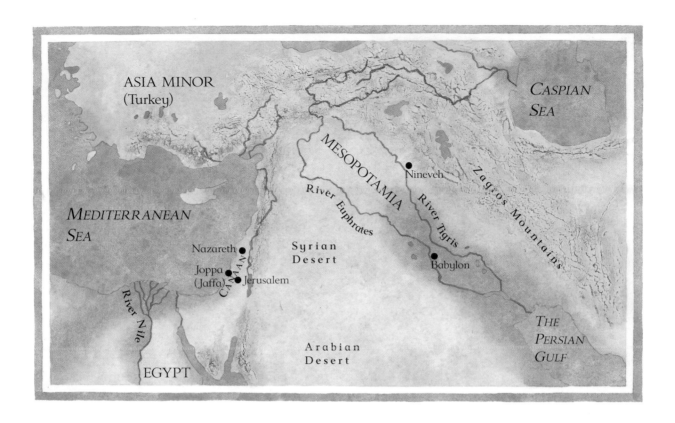

A book of miracles

The Book of Jonah is full of miracles, events that could not happen without God's help. There is the storm, the vine that grows in a night and dies in the night and, perhaps most amazingly, the way Jonah's life is saved by a large fish. What type of fish could it be? The Bible gives us no clues. However, some people have suggested that it was not a fish but a sperm whale. These huge animals do occasionally swim in the Mediterranean and it might be possible for one to swallow a man whole. Even so, it is still a miracle that Jonah survived his experience.

Useful words

Fast To fast means to choose not to eat and so go hungry. Most religions ask people to fast at times so that they can focus on their religious beliefs and their relationship with God rather than on their everyday lives.

Hebrew The Hebrews were an ancient people from the Middle East region of Asia. The Jewish religion began amongst the Hebrews, who are also sometimes called the Children of Israel. Most of the Old Testament of the Bible was originally written in the Hebrew language.

Drawing lots Drawing lots is a way people make a choice or decision by chance, particularly when choosing one person from a group. The lots are a collection of long thin objects of different lengths, such as slips of wood or straws. Someone holds the ends of the lots in his or her hand so that their length can not be seen. Then each person in the group takes, or draws, a lot from the hand. The person who draws the shortest lot is then selected.

Mercy To show mercy is to hold back from punishing someone for doing something wrong. It is kind to show mercy and often part of forgiving.

Pray When people pray they talk to God, to worship Him, to ask Him for help and guidance and to feel close to Him. Praying is an important part of both the Jewish and Christian religions. Some prayers are said out loud in a group, others are said on your own, quietly or in your head.

Prophet In the Bible, a prophet is someone who has a special relationship with God. God spoke directly to the prophets and they passed His messages and commands to other people. Some of the prophets also saw into the future and told people, or prophesied, what might happen.